LEADING FOR LIFE
10 STORIES OF GOD'S TRANSFORMATIONAL POWER

SUE CURRANS FULTZ

ISBN: 978-0-9972285-1-9

Care Net
www.care-net.org
44180 Riverside Parkway, Suite 200
Lansdowne, VA 20176
Phone: 703-554-8734
Fax: 703-554-8735
Email: info@care-net.org

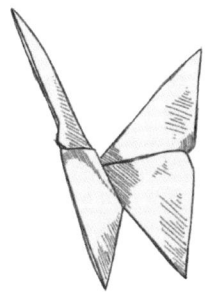

DEDICATION

This life-honoring book is dedicated to the life and memory of little David, my precious four-year-old grandson, whose life was cut short by a malignant brain tumor. He reminded us that every life, no matter how short, is a sacred, amazing gift from God and a precious treasure, profoundly impacting us and our world. This book is also dedicated to all the unborn children whose lives have ended prematurely by abortion or by miscarriage. Every life matters to us— the human family—and every life matters to our Heavenly Father.

What an amazing record of those who have been dedicated and those that are still working to save and honor life and the lives of the unborn. The leadership insights are valuable to all who read and implement them.

Stephen Arterburn,
Author and founder of New Life LIVE

The onslaught of attacks and dehumanization on the unborn is the greatest cause of our generation and all generations after us until it ends. This powerful book shows that leaders in this beautiful mission must put God first and inspire those around them to be their brothers' keeper.

Shawn D. Carney
President & CEO of 40 Days for Life
Bestselling author of *The Beginning of the End of Abortion* and *To the Heart of the Matter*

The timing of this book is perfect! As America approaches the 50th anniversary of *Roe v. Wade* and the next generation is putting its hand to the plow, what better subject than *Leading For Life* and what better author than someone who has been there and fought the fight?

Kent Ostrander
Executive Director, The Family Foundation (KY)

When God told Moses to set His people free, Moses had no idea how it would happen. When God wants something done, he chooses those who don't know what they're doing! These wonderful leaders, by their obedience, have enabled God to work through them. Let's be inspired by their example!

Fr. Frank Pavone, National Director, Priests for Life
President, National Pro-life Religious Council
Pastoral Director, Silent No More and Rachel's Vineyard

Leading for Life highlights the inspiring trailblazers that helped launch a movement of LIFE. Sue Fultz delivers the moving stories beautifully. This book is an insightful tool that will inspire and equip every pro-life leader!

Amy Ford
President, Embrace Grace, Inc

Every Christian needs to read the author's heart-gripping and spiritually-challenging true-life testimonies. The body of Christ cannot ignore the pain and guilt induced by abortion. Thank God for Sue and Care Net, who exemplify the essence of the Gospel, "giving individuals a future not dictated by the past."

Darius Salter Ph. D.
Former Executive Director of the Christian Holiness Association,
Pastor, seminary teacher, and author of nine books

The stories of my heroes in *Leading for Life* are so inspiring! I highly recommend this book for anyone serving in the compassionate side of our movement. The leadership insights, prayers and applications at the end of each chapter would be great morning devotions for pregnancy centers."

Linda Cochrane, RN
CEO, Hopeline Pregnancy Resource Center, Care Net Specialist, author of *Forgiven and*
Set Free

Heroes are often unsung—and yet they exist. These are the ones who live out courage, hope and servanthood in their leadership. Heroes often do not tell their own stories, but Sue does—her book inspires us all to stay on the journey for life!

Kathleen Patterson, PhD
Professor and Doctoral Program Director, Regent University

Sue Fultz tells, in dramatic fashion, stories that exemplify that pro-life workers, through unconditional love and courageous action, help "abortion-minded" women and men choose life for their unborn babies. Honoring these who also provide hope and recovery for those experiencing abortion regret, Sue reminds us that every life matters to God.

W. David Hager, M.D., FACOG
Baptist Health Medical Group, Women's Care
Focus on the Family, Physicians Resource Council

Leading for Life is a must-read, Sue really captures the heart and passion behind the leaders. Pro-life workers are on a frontline battle and these stories provide encouragement and wisdom for weary soldiers. When you understand a person's story then you can really understand the passion.

Lisa A. Maloney, LMFT
President of the CT Pregnancy Care Coalition and Executive Director of Care Net
Pregnancy Resource Center of Southeastern CT

You can't read *Leading for Life* without being inspired by the beautiful God stories of these leaders in our life movement. The common theme of God taking broken people and using their brokenness to impact life now and for eternity will empower you to trust God will use your brokenness for His glorious purpose.

Marsha Middleton
CEO, Alliance for Life - Missouri

The passage in Hebrews 12:1 of the 'great cloud of witnesses' came to mind when reading Sue's book. Battling in this opposed fight, it is easy to feel isolated. However, this book is a beautiful reminder that we are surrounded by others and it rises up in me bravery to keep gaining ground.

Laura Dickinson,
Executive Director of Clarity Solutions,
President of the Kentucky Association of Pregnancy Care Agencies (KAPCA)

Amazing pioneers of the pregnancy center movement! So very important that their stories are captured, their legacies spotlighted. Sue Fultz has given just the right combination of honoring them . . . but more importantly giving the glory to the Lord they served at every step of the way.

Bobbie Meyer
State Director, LifeLink Carolina, the North Carolina State Coalition

May these testimonies serve to ignite faith in all who feel God's call to bring His solutions to our land. And in the words of Anne Pierson, may you "hear God's heart for [you] and his call on [your life]—and be inspired and have the courage to make a difference for him."

Laura Lewis, MD, CCFP
Executive Director, Pregnancy Care Canada

TABLE OF CONTENTS

FOREWORD

I am come that they might have life, and that they may have it more abundantly.

—John 10:10

Some books beg to be written. Sue Fultz has written just such a book. It's a book of stories, representing a tiny fraction of the powerful stories God has been writing among life-affirming leaders. These leaders labor, typically in obscurity, to bring Christ-centered compassion, hope, and help to people in their communities considering abortion, and the impact of their work will only be fully recognized from eternity.

Recognizing God as the author of the story has been very important in my own life and leadership. Looking back, I'm amazed at how our Heavenly Father has woven his grace into my life story, using even my not-so-great choices for his glory.

When I was around seven years old, I lost my father, not to death, but to divorce. As a result, my mother found herself responsible for four small children when she was in her early twenties. Our life was difficult. She did her very best to support us, and, although we didn't have a dad in our lives, she always made sure we knew that the ideal was a dad and a mom, loving each other and loving their children together.

I wanted more from life than what I'd experienced, and so I worked very hard as a teen. Given my background, it was extraordinary that I had the opportunity to attend Princeton University.

It was there that I met Yvette. I was a sophomore, and since we both lived in the same dorm and ate at the same cafeteria, it wasn't long before I noticed her. I wanted to meet her, but nothing seemed to be working out. One rainy evening after I left football practice, I finally got the courage to just walk alongside her. When she looked up at me, I said, "What's a nice girl like you doing out on a night like this?" While she later told me that was pretty corny, it worked!

I learned that her mother had passed away after a battle with cancer the summer before Yvette's senior year of high school. During that painful experience, Yvette felt God was calling her into the medical field. When she graduated, she was thrilled to be accepted at Princeton to pursue her dream of becoming a doctor. I shared my dreams with her, too. We really connected, spending much of our time outside of class together.

Soon, we were in love. We shared faith in Jesus Christ and we knew that marriage was God's intended context for sexual intimacy. But we made choices that compromised our convictions. During the first half of our sophomore year, we kept getting closer, including sexually. Then we went home to spend Christmas with our families. Just a few days into Christmas break, Yvette called to tell me that she thought she was pregnant. You can imagine our shock . . . and our fears.

After we returned from Christmas break, Yvette went to Princeton's student health center for a pregnancy test. She remembers exactly what the nurse said after confirming that she was pregnant: "Yvette, you are going to have an abortion, aren't you?" Yvette told the nurse no—she wanted to get married and have her baby. When Yvette said that she was a sophomore and planned to be a doctor, the nurse wasn't encouraging. "How are you going to graduate with a child?" she asked. Abortion was the only option she offered to Yvette.

That could have been the beginning of the end of our story. But instead of driving us apart, our child brought us together. When we talked after Yvette's visit with the nurse, something changed. It was like the whole thing was in slow motion because it was such a life-defining moment. I told Yvette we would get married as planned. We chose life and we chose marriage.

As Christians in a community of Christians, we also knew that there were going to be difficult and embarrassing conversations ahead. The first person we told was my mother. She was deeply disappointed and worried that a baby meant I would drop out of college and risk my future. Telling Yvette's dad was even harder. When her pregnancy started showing at four months, she wrote him a letter. Her dad called and told her he loved her and didn't want her to get married unless that's what she truly wanted. She could come home. But, he said, if we did get married, we would have to be adults and support ourselves.

So, we were married by the justice of the peace with just a few college friends as witnesses. Help was sparse that summer, and there was no transitional housing. I stayed on campus to work and practice for the coming football season. Yvette went home to Texas for the summer, and I joined her for the birth of our son in September. We named him Jamin.

By God's grace, our unplanned family was part of his perfect plan for our lives. The nurse who confirmed Yvette's pregnancy had questioned how she could graduate while caring for a child. In fact, Yvette graduated from Princeton with two children. Our youngest son, Justin, was conceived in her senior year and born just a couple of weeks before her thesis was due. She had two deliveries at the same time—a baby and a thesis. An Associated Press reporter printed a photo of a happy Yvette carrying little Justin at her Princeton graduation. We did it together and I was so proud of her.

I began my career in business while Yvette took time off to parent our sons. But we never gave up on her dream, and she went on to become a physician. She has served as the medical director and a board member for a local pregnancy center and still practices medicine today, serving a population that is mostly elderly and rural.

When I look back, abortion could have seemed easier. We could have tried to pretend Jamin hadn't happened and gotten on with the lives we had planned. But making the decision to be a husband to Yvette and a father to my son was the best choice I could have ever made. God gave me the grace and wisdom to do that even as a twenty-year-old.

Becoming a father was a defining moment for me. God kept giving me opportunities to help other guys with fatherhood while I was still learning how to be a father myself.

I got my MBA and spent decades in corporate America: Goldman Sachs, PepsiCo, IBM. All this time, God was preparing me to serve in a different way. I made the switch to nonprofit leadership in 2001, when I was named president of the National Fatherhood Initiative. There, I was driven to help men be better dads and to reduce father absence through the creation of practical, evidence-based resources.

In 2012, the Care Net board of directors asked me to become Care Net's CEO and president. Leading the organization's more than eleven hundred affiliate pregnancy centers has been the greatest privilege of my professional life. My passion is to advocate not just for life, but for a fresh, pro-abundant-life vision in our culture and movement!

Soon after joining Care Net, I commissioned new research into the experience of women who had experienced abortion.[1] The research found that when a woman becomes pregnant unexpectedly, the first person she tells is usually the baby's father. And four out of ten women who experience abortion do so while attending church, at least monthly. To ensure no one would feel trapped into an unwanted abortion, I knew Care Net had to do more than ever before to help women—and men too. I led an initiative to help pregnancy centers intentionally welcome new dads and equip them to make their own decisions for life. When couples make this decision together and have the support they need, it's more likely not only that their babies will be born, but that they will be born into loving families.

And whether they are parenting alone or together, new moms and dads need a supportive community. Most of all, they need an opportunity to encounter abundant life through Jesus Christ. So I led Care Net in a groundbreaking initiative called Making Life Disciples. This program empowers churches to support new parents facing pregnancy decisions and to embrace pregnancy center clients with ongoing support and discipleship.

God took me from a fatherless home to places of influence. In 2015, Newsmax included me among its "100 Most Influential Pro-Life Advocates." Today, my passion is to see the next generation of pro-life leaders equipped for excellence in ministry and service. I started doing "Life Chat" videos to share how principles I've learned as a business leader can inspire nonprofit success. And Care Net launched Centers of Excellence University to provide state-of-the-art online professional development for pregnancy centers. We are doing this for the exact same reasons that I am excited about this book: because God delights in using his people to lead and inspire others in making transformational differences in their communities.

My story is unique, but it isn't exceptional. If you are in Christ, then I'm confident that God is using your unique story too, and he's doing it right now, in ways you may—or may not—be aware of.

In this book, my friend Sue tells the stories of how God has used leaders not

1 Care Net. *Study of Women Who Have Had an Abortion and Their Views on Church.* Lansdowne, VA: Care Net, n.d. https://drive.google.com/file/d/0B-O7y15KcvyWajdWX181ZXNkRWc/view.

too different from us. I hope you will be encouraged and equipped in your own leadership journey as you read the pages ahead.

Yours for abundant life,
Roland C. Warren

HOW DO YOU LIVE IT?

1. What does abundant life mean to you?
2. How does Jesus give abundant life?

INTRODUCTION

Thomas A. Glessner, JD, President
National Institute of Family and Life Advocates (NIFLA)

In 1979, when I was a young lawyer in Seattle, the Lord shook both my wife and me to the core. We became aware of the issue of abortion and its serious implications for the future.

Our passions and convictions led us to start the first "crisis pregnancy center" (as such agencies were called then) in the Pacific Northwest. I became its founding board chair.

This deep passion led me to eventually leave my law practice and become CEO of the Christian Action Council, now Care Net, in Washington, DC. Five years later I became the founder and CEO of NIFLA.

Over these many years in pro-life ministry, I have become acquainted with true unsung American heroes—leaders of pregnancy center ministries. They have given up fame and fortune to serve the very least of our brethren, the unborn. I am honored to call these saints my friends.

Sue Fultz has done an outstanding job in sharing the remarkable lives of just a few of these heroes. You will be inspired by their stories.

Pregnancy centers have been vilified by those who support abortion. However, as these stories indicate, one day the work of pregnancy center leaders will be honored when they hear, "Well done, my good and faithful servant."

PREFACE

There are heroes among us—and they are leading for life.

For decades God has been advancing the cause for life across our nation. He has been calling followers of Christ, one by one, to lead in this great movement, writing the pro-abundant-life story through them. This is a book of their stories—and most of all, it is a book of his-story.

These are stories of commitment, sacrifice, and courage. They are stories of supernatural God encounters, God's calling, and his anointing. These men and women are just a few of those who are daily serving families making pregnancy decisions. They work on the front lines of this movement quietly, faithfully, and with great perseverance.

As a Care Net center services specialist, almost daily I hear incredible stories about pro-life leaders. And in my role as a national consultant and trainer, I have traveled to many centers and spoken with hundreds of these leaders. I have seen firsthand the work they are doing. Without exception, their stories are God stories!

One common thread is that, first and foremost, these leaders are serving the God they love. Out of their hearts for him flow their compassion, hope, and help. They know he has called them. He has given them the leadership characteristics that enable them to lead their ministries. And they give him all the glory.

Called by God as servants to care for his children who are hurting, they have amazing stories of his grace, provision, and miracles. Remember, the Bible itself is a book of stories, together telling one story—his-story! The leaders in the biblical account—as well as the leaders in these pro-life stories—were ordinary, often flawed, individuals. But because of their obedience to God's call, they became great leaders who inspired generations.

God still calls the ordinary to accomplish the extraordinary, and he gets the glory. Like the disciples of Jesus who said, "As for us, we cannot help speaking about what we have seen and heard" (Acts 4:20), pro-life workers cannot stop telling about what they have seen and heard, that God might be glorified.

We praise him that this powerful movement continues to sweep across our nation, through those he has called! He writes their story.

It is my hope that you will be encouraged and inspired by the life-affirming work of these leaders. I pray you will learn from the leadership characteristics they exemplify. I know you will be in awe of God's presence and transformational power in their lives.

As you read their stories, remember it is God who is writing the story. Remember, too, your calling and your God-given characteristics. I fervently

pray that you will be inspired to join in his-story for life.

1 | **PRIORITIZING JESUS**
THE SOL PITCHON STORY

But seek first his kingdom and his righteousness, and all these things
will be given to you as well.

—Matthew 6:33

Sixteen-year-old Garmaine lay on a surgical table as a Nazi doctor removed one ovary. Before the doctor could remove her other ovary, the Allied forces began dropping bombs and the doctor ran for cover.

An imprisoned Jewish doctor was told to finish the procedure. "Young lady," the doctor said to Garmaine, "I am going to have to make an incision, but I am not going to remove your ovary. However, I ask you to do two things. I want you to hide your monthly cycle and to name your first child after me."

Garmaine, her mother, and her four sisters had arrived at the Auschwitz concentration camp after eight days in a crowded cattle car with no food or water. Garmaine's mother and sisters were immediately taken to the gas chamber. Garmaine was placed in block ten, the infamous medical experimentation block. Young women in this block were subjected to inhumane, often fatal, experimental procedures. Garmaine had been chosen for surgical sterilization—prevented only by falling bombs and the Jewish doctor.

Garmaine survived Auschwitz for nearly three more years before she was freed. Years later, when her first child was born, she gave him the doctor's name: Solomon Samuel.

This child, Sol Pitchon, grew up to be president and CEO of New Life Solutions in Largo, Florida. "My mother survived the Holocaust of World War II," Sol says. "Now God has me serving him against the holocaust of abortion in America today."

Sol was born to Garmaine and Simon (another Holocaust survivor) in Greece, far from America and the holocaust of abortion. Daily, Sol's mother would go to the consulate and show her concentration camp tattoo (#41570), requesting to go to America. Finally the consul said, "OK. You leave for America in one week."

Sol's family first settled in Ohio, but in 1958 they moved to Florida, where Sol lives today. They were cultural Jews and occasionally went to the synagogue. Sol didn't think much about God until he was ten, when, walking past a church, he clearly heard God say to his heart, "We live forever."

Sol didn't understand what that meant, but he never forgot.

Sol had his first encounter with a Jewish believer when he was in his mid-thirties, married with children, and working in the insurance and investment field. He paid a visit to an affluent Jewish man named Mark to try to sell him investment products. As soon as Sol walked into Mark's office, Mark said, "I'm glad to meet you, Sol. I am a Jewish believer. I believe in Jesus."

Wow! What did I get myself into? thought Sol. But as the two talked, Sol saw a peace and joy in Mark that he wanted.

Mark told Sol that one's identity is in Christ alone. Mark was successful and affluent. "But," he said, "if I lost everything, it wouldn't matter. All I need is Jesus." Mark had lost much already; when he became a believer, his family disowned him and actually had a funeral. Sol was impressed by how Mark had made Jesus his first priority.

Sol and his family visited Mark's church in June 1981, and during the altar call, Sol went forward. However, he never went back to that church. Jesus had become Sol's Savior, but because Sol did not receive discipleship, Jesus was not his Lord nor his priority.

In June 1982, Sol's wife left their marriage. Sol was crushed. He went into a deep, six-month depression. With many people praying for him, he came out of that depression with a heart for the Lord. He started attending church and began growing in his faith. He says, "I never looked back—never!"

At church, Sol met Terri, who had also gone through an unwanted divorce. Terri told Sol that during a crisis in her marriage, she had had an abortion.

Sol believed abortion was "a woman's choice." But his view changed when Terri told him about the sanctity of life and invited him to pray with her at a

St. Petersburg abortion clinic. In front of that clinic, Sol had his first encounter with the pro-life movement—an encounter that would change his life!

Sol and Terri married and began to support New Life Solutions Pregnancy Center. In 1998, the center's president and CEO, Raul Reyes, relocated. He told Sol that God had shown him Sol was to take his place as CEO.

At the time, Sol was a partner in a Christian psychotherapy practice, and his first response was, "No way!" But Terri was ecstatic about this new opportunity. Sol agreed to fast and pray about it, and God clearly confirmed this was part of his calling to make Jesus his first priority. In January 1999, Sol became the CEO of New Life Solutions.

New Life Solutions has had a phenomenal pro-life impact. The ministry, which operates four medical clinics, has reached over 100,000 clients and their families, rescued nearly 10,000 unborn babies, educated over 180,000 youth about avoiding risky sexual behavior, and rejoiced in nearly 9,000 professions of faith. They have ministered to hundreds of single moms and children through their residential program. They have served thousands of men, women, and teens in their abortion recovery program and have had over 1,400 births at their accredited birth and midwifery practice.

In 2018, Sol and the board of directors implemented a succession plan, bringing on Charles DiMarco as the new president and CEO of New Life Solutions. Sol began transitioning into his new role of vice president of church and community partnerships. He envisions New Life Solutions equipping other centers and helping them make an even greater difference in their communities and in the pro-life movement.

Sol has become a well-known leader and mentor. He has inspired thousands as a speaker at pregnancy center banquets and state and national conferences and through his testimony on CBN's *The 700 Club*. He has been honored by Care Net, Heartbeat International, and the Florida Family Policy Council. Sol has helped train countless leaders, including the founders of Cree Women's Care, the first pregnancy center in Puerto Rico.

Sol emphasizes that leadership isn't a solo activity. His Christ-centered, servant-leadership style is led by the Holy Spirit with a focus on connecting with others. "In 2018," he shares, "I attended my twentieth Care Net conference. I am so grateful to Care Net because it has been such a huge part of my growth and of all I have learned and all that has been accomplished in my pro-life ministry experience."

In May 2019, Sol and two friends were flying in a pontoon plane in Alaska. During their landing approach in Prince William Sound, the wheels touched the water and the plane flipped.

All three men were knocked unconscious. When Sol regained consciousness, the cabin was filling with water and he had to quit breathing. But then he looked up and saw a light. He swam toward it, praying that the Lord would provide him enough air to reach it. Scott, the pilot, was standing on the airplane's wing. He grabbed Sol's hands as he broke the surface of the water and pulled him up—saving him from drowning.

Scott kept saying, "Bill didn't make it! Bill didn't make it!" Their friend, Bill, had died in the crash.

Severely injured, Sol waited four hours with Scott for a Coast Guard helicopter to pick them up and take them to the Providence Alaska Medical Center in Anchorage. Sol had multiple crushed ribs, his left lung had to be drained of accumulated water and blood, and he underwent spinal surgery to fuse six vertebrae. Sol needed a body brace from morning till night for many months and received intense physical therapy to help him walk again.

As a life-affirming leader, Sol says this experience has intensified his passion and love for the Lord. "The Lord has given me another chance in life. My heart has become even more determined to help bring an end to the holocaust of abortion that is killing our nation!"

Sol would say that the hand of God has orchestrated circumstances and people, guiding him to fight our country's holocaust. A Jewish doctor made Sol's life possible. Sol's leadership has made life possible for many children, and through his leadership, thousands of families have been transformed by the gospel of Jesus Christ. All of this has come about as a result of Sol putting Jesus first.

LEADERSHIP INSIGHT

I have been crucified with Christ and I no longer live, but Christ lives in me. The life I now live in the body, I live by faith in the Son of God, who loved me and gave himself for me.

—Galatians 2:20

The God of the universe knew Jeremiah before he was formed in his mother's womb (Jeremiah 1:5). That same God knew Sol before he was even conceived. God knew Sol when his mother was on the operating table, when the bombs dropped, and when the Jewish doctor saved her ovary. God intervened throughout Sol's life to lead him in God's own plan and purpose. God knew Sol, and one day, Sol came to know God.

As a follower of Christ and a leader of people, Sol lives and breathes this reality: "I have been crucified with Christ and I no longer live, but Christ lives in me."

"Somewhere along the line," Sol says, "I totally gave my heart, future, and everything to Jesus. Jesus said, 'You are going to work at the pregnancy center! Don't get hung up on opening more Christian therapy offices. You are on assignment!' All Terri and I knew was that we wanted to honor God and put Jesus first."

Prioritizing Jesus changed the trajectory of Sol Pitchon's life. It can change yours, too. In fact, if you are to be the leader your team needs, you must prioritize Jesus.

LET'S PRAY:

Thank you, God, that you know us! You have a purpose and a plan for us. Thank you for orchestrating our lives in amazing ways and giving us all we need as we serve you in pro-life ministry and as we make Jesus our first priority. Amen.

HOW DO YOU LIVE IT?

1. Read Sol's story. Highlight the times when God intervened to direct his life to Jesus and to his calling as a pro-life leader.

2. List the times that God has intervened to direct you to him and to what he is calling you to do.

3. In what way does Galatians 2:20 speak to you about your life's priority?

4. God interrupted Sol's plans for building a therapy practice. How do you respond to divine interruptions to your plans?

2 | **PASSION**
THE ANDY MERRITT STORY

Then I heard the voice of the Lord saying, "Whom shall I send, and
who will go for us?" And I said, "Here am I. Send me!"

—Isaiah 6:8

"God's presence just came into that stairwell . . ." Andy Merritt's voice chokes with emotion. "It is always difficult to share this part. I had an overwhelming sense of his presence—a feeling of great fear at being drawn into the presence of a holy God." In this powerful, extraordinary encounter in the spring of 1972, God called Andy Merritt to pro-life ministry.

Andy, now a pro-life leader and senior pastor of Edgewood Baptist Church in Columbus, Georgia, came to know Christ only a year and a half before this dramatic God encounter. He came to God in great brokenness out of a life of sin and rebellion. When he met Jesus, his life was transformed.

Andy entered Bible college in the Washington, DC, area. During his sophomore year, as he was studying in the college library below the chapel, Andy heard the choir practicing. Caught up in the beauty of the music, he went to study in the stairwell between the library and the chapel, where he could hear the choir's music clearly.

The choir began to sing, "Take my life and let it be consecrated, Lord, to thee . . ." Andy had never heard that hymn before, and the words captured him. The last verse expressed the cry of his heart: "Take my will and make it Thine . . . . Take my heart . . . it shall be Thy royal throne." As Andy began to pray those words, God supernaturally came into the stairwell. "I literally thought I was going to die," Andy says now.

That night, Andy sought solitude in the small church where he was the youth pastor, and in that quietness, God showed Andy his calling and destiny. Through Scripture, God revealed to Andy how, when a nation forsakes God, it falls into the path of God's judgment. The first step is always idolatry—the forsaking of God. This path then leads to immorality and self-gratification, because once God is eliminated, there is no basis for moral absolutes. God opened Andy's eyes to see where America was on this path. The next inevitable step would be inhumanity.

Andy left the church that night with this calling from God: "I want you to establish arks of refuge for those who are doomed to death by the inhumanity of your age." Only twenty years old and a relatively new Christian, Andy understood that this was his destiny. Although he didn't know what it fully meant and knew nothing about abortion, he clearly saw that the nation was about to step into inhumanity.

Andy will never be able to escape the three truths that God drove into his heart that night. God said, "Andy, to conquer in ministry you must be Christ's captive; you should never focus on success in ministry, but on the holiness of heart and life; and finally, Andy, your weakness will be my opportunity to display my strength." With those words, God placed a burning passion in Andy's heart for the calling he had given him.

Many evenings of tears followed, during which Andy had no words to express his inescapable burden. God was showing him that the first step into his calling needed to be fervent prayer.

The next year, on January 22, 1973, *Roe v. Wade* legalized abortion. Meanwhile, Andy graduated from college and married his wife, Kathy, and they began church planting in Delaware. After a few years, the couple moved to Columbus, Georgia, where Andy became one of the pastors at Edgewood Baptist Church. He continued to carry the burden God had placed on his heart.

In 1979, the film series *Whatever Happened to the Human Race?* came to Atlanta. It was based on the book by Francis Schaeffer—a favorite author of Andy's—and C. Everett Koop, who became surgeon general under President Ronald Reagan. The two authors had collaborated on the project to show how the gospel should influence Christians' understanding of abortion, infanticide, euthanasia, and secular humanism.

Andy and Kathy attended the film series. That is when God clarified that the calling he had placed on Andy's life was to the unborn. God told him, "Andy, this is the inhumanity of your age. These are the little ones for whom I want you to establish arks of refuge to save their lives."

Andy began challenging his church to stand in the gap for those doomed to death by the inhumanity of abortion. The church developed a plan to establish "arks of refuge"—then called crisis pregnancy centers. These centers would provide women with free pregnancy tests along with education about the sanctity of human life and the realities of abortion, all embedded in the gospel. Through this model, women experiencing pregnancy as a crisis would have the opportunity to choose life for their babies and eternal life for themselves.

In March 1981, Edgewood opened a pregnancy ministry that operated out of Andy's office. Women would come to the church office, provide urine samples, and receive educational literature. A local ob-gyn tested each sample. When the women called to get their test results, Andy would also invite them back to receive assistance.

The pregnancy center operated on this model for eighteen months. Amazingly, it had twelve hundred contacts and ministered to about four hundred women. God was working miracles!

In the fall of 1982, the pregnancy center opened in a separate facility—and the ministry literally exploded. The number of clients dramatically increased; soon the center was averaging over one hundred pregnancy tests per week. The center began to experience media attacks. But God just kept blessing.

All over the nation, people began to hear about what was happening in Georgia and to ask for help starting other centers. Seeing the potential for expanding this type of ministry, Andy sought solitude in a small cabin for an entire week, fasting and praying, seeking God's guidance. That week, Andy wrote the ministry's first operational manual to train pregnancy center workers.

Andy began travelling across the country to help establish pregnancy centers and train staff and volunteers. In the ensuing years, he helped start and developed relationships with five hundred centers. Later, those centers would affiliate with even larger networks of centers—Care Net, Heartbeat International, and the National Institute of Family and Life Advocates.

In the mid-1980s, Edgewood began hosting free national conferences every two years with the goal of giving center workers a hero's welcome. Over the years, thousands of pregnancy center staff and volunteers have been blessed by attending.

As hostility toward centers has increased, Andy believes God is seeking center workers who will trust completely in him. Andy is passionate about preparing centers to recognize how God is using the worsening storm of opposition to define and increase their ministry. He challenges pro-life workers, "Do not retreat! Advance as never before! Regardless of the price, in spite of persecution, prepare to follow, honor, and suffer for Jesus."

LEADERSHIP INSIGHT

I cling to you; your right hand upholds me.

—Psalm 63:8

An encounter with the holy God fueled a passion for him in Andy Merritt's heart. That passion drove Andy to cling to God, and to seek a life and ministry in which this holy God would increase and he would decrease. The passion God put in Andy's heart that night continues to burn today.

Passion for God is a powerful leadership characteristic. It empowers leaders to accomplish what is beyond their own ability and to reach into the miraculous.

This is not just Andy's story, it is God's story. As pro-abundant-life workers, we know that "with God all things are possible" (Matthew 19:26). With him we can establish arks of refuge to save the lives of little ones and offer their parents abundant life through Jesus Christ.

> Cling to God. That passion for him will accomplish and fulfill your calling and destiny, and he will receive glory.

LET'S PRAY:

Thank you, Father, for our high and holy calling. Our souls cling to you. Thank you for holding us up with your mighty right hand. All things are possible when we abide in you. May you receive all the glory. In Jesus' name, amen.

HOW DO YOU LIVE IT?

1. Who is the object of Andy's passion?

2. How is Andy's passion demonstrated in his life?

3. How would you describe the passion God has placed in your heart?

3 | VISION & OBEDIENCE
THE RAUL & CHRISTINE REYES STORY

He said to them, "Go into all the world and preach the gospel to all creation."
—Mark 16:15

Soon after they were married, Raul and Christine Reyes heard Jesus say, "Go!"

It was 1982, and the book *Whatever Happened to the Human Race?* by Francis Schaeffer and C. Everett Koop had just opened Raul's and Christine's eyes to the abortion issue. Christine was pregnant with their first child when they realized that, every day, babies like theirs were being killed by abortion. They sensed God's call to dedicate their lives to upholding the sanctity of life by speaking up for the unborn and sharing the gospel. Together, Raul and Christine committed to be obedient to God's call and this vision for their lives.

God opened the door for them to answer his call to "Go" when, in 1983, they were asked to help start the first pregnancy center in Florida. They worked on its founding board for two years, and then Raul became the president. The center, now called New Life Solutions, grew to include five locations and a birthing center.

In the years that followed, God gave the Reyeses four beautiful children, and life seemed perfect. Then Christine became pregnant again. This time, the couple's finances, small home, and energy seemed to have extended as far as possible. After dedicating her life to encouraging women to choose life for their babies, now Christine was experiencing a pregnancy that she did not want.

When Michael was born in 1992, Christine knew something was different. He wasn't like her other children. Michael had difficulty nursing, his development was slow, he slept for only a couple of hours a night, and he didn't hit the typical milestones. Christine's heart broke when he didn't smile at all. She told God she could handle Michael's physical issues, but not this! She was tired, emotionally spent, and angry with God for giving her this child with mental limitations.

"God loved me in spite of my heart condition," Christine now says. In his grace, he used a simple phone call to begin to change her heart. A friend who was a single mom with one son called to share with Christine her excitement that God was allowing her to adopt a child with Down syndrome—a child no one else wanted. Christine was so convicted she fell on her knees and wept.

Later that day as she was sitting and crying, Christine felt suspended in time. She distinctly heard a voice say, "You are blessed to have this child." She believed it was an angel bringing her a message from the Lord that she should not fear; God would take care of everything. Slowly she began to accept that her son was a gift.

As Michael grew, so did his list of challenges: severe asthma, poor muscle tone, poor eyesight, inability to communicate, and other developmental issues. But after many emotional years of helping Michael survive, Christine and Raul now say he is the joy of their lives. They thank God for this special child, who has brought them to a deeper understanding of the value of every human life. They know from experience that an unexpected child with unwelcome difficulties can bring immeasurable joy.

In 1999 they were asked to join the Pregnancy Resource Center (PRC) in Grand Rapids, Michigan. Raul became the director of international ministries, helping start and train pregnancy centers around the world, while Christine led the international ministry events. Eventually the PRC's international work (called LIFE International) became an independent ministry, and Raul and Christine continued their service at the national and international levels, helping expand pregnancy centers throughout the globe.

Raul and Christine then felt called to Colorado, where Raul served as an assistant to Dr. James Dobson at Focus on the Family and Chris became executive director of the Colorado Springs Pregnancy Center (CSPC). Christine grew the CSPC significantly, and eventually Raul joined her as president while Christine continued in her role as executive director. They changed the name of the center to Life Network and expanded its scope with programs for youth relationships and sexual risk avoidance, prenatal health, and abortion recovery.

In 2014 God called Raul and Christine to Phoenix, where Raul served as president and Christine once again served as executive director of the four Choices Pregnancy Centers. Their time in Arizona ended in 2019 when they returned to Colorado to be close to family and to launch an international ministry called Life Equip Global. Christine returned to a leadership role at Life Network.

Raul and Christine have now been serving in the abortion mission field for thirty-seven years. Michael, now twenty-seven years old, has made this journey with them. They often bring him with them to conferences and speaking engagements in America as well as on international trips. He continues to inspire and motivate his parents. And God tenderly uses Michael's presence as a witness to the value and beauty of life—that he has a plan and purpose for every person.

"The thread that runs through all we have done is the gospel," Raul says. "There is nothing that comes close to that." Depending on Christ and each other, the couple says their pro-life work is simply a long walk in the same direction, following Christ.

Today, God's expanded vision for them is to take the gospel into the abortion mission field all around the world. They are laying the foundation for their next endeavor, Life Equip Global. Their vision is to use technology to equip believers around the world to defend life and share the gospel. Raul and Christine continue to be obedient to the vision God has given them.

Abortion, Raul says, is a global holocaust. He believes that when we view abortion only from the perspective of saving babies, we miss a bigger picture. Abortion isn't only an act of individual desperation. It is part of a strategic, global assault on life. That assault is a physical reflection of the spiritual assault on God perpetrated by the evil one. Raul encourages pro-life leaders to recognize that their local battle is part of this global struggle.

Looking back, Raul and Christine realize that the Lord has always been preparing them for this global work. His call to "Go" took them across the United States, from Florida to Michigan, Colorado, and Arizona, and to thirty-four countries. Now, he is releasing them with fresh vision and anointing to share the gospel in the mission field created by abortion—anywhere in the world.

LEADERSHIP INSIGHT

So then, King Agrippa, I was not disobedient to the vision from heaven.

—Acts 26:19

Raul and Christine's vision and obedience have equipped them to understand and go whenever and wherever God calls them. Today, they are prepared to spiritually understand the evil one's strategic global assault on life and to expand their ministry "into all the world."

Leading for life is a grand spiritual calling, and each of us on this mission field must rely on God for a vision of where he desires us to serve. Leaders must be obedient to the vision and understand that the struggle is not against flesh and blood but against the powers of this dark world.

As leaders, we must know and be obedient to God's vision; and we must understand and take a stand against the devil's schemes.

LET'S PRAY:

Father, we pray that we will be strong in the Lord and put on the full armor of God. Open our eyes to see your vision. We will stand firm. Whenever we speak, give us the words to say, that we may fearlessly make known the mystery of the gospel. In Jesus' name and to the glory of God, amen.

HOW DO YOU LIVE IT?

1. How are Christine and Raul's vision and obedience seen in their life journey?

2. In what ways are vision and obedience important to you as you lead for life?

3. Write a prayer asking God to help you see and be obedient to his vision for leadership.

4 | HOPE
THE GWEN KIK STORY

Not only so, but we also glory in our sufferings, because we know that suffering produces perseverance; perseverance, character; and character, hope. And hope does not put us to shame, because God's love has been poured out into our hearts through the Holy Spirit, who has been given to us.

—Romans 5:3–5

It was January 22, 1993, the twentieth anniversary of *Roe v. Wade*. Gwen Kik was listening to NPR on her car radio when she heard a woman's voice that sounded familiar—"like when you hear your mother's voice and you stop to listen," Gwen says. Gwen turned up the radio to "stop to listen."

The woman was talking about a pregnancy center, and Gwen's heart started to pound. She had never heard of this kind of center. But at that moment, Gwen knew she was supposed to start one in her hometown of Madisonville, Kentucky.

The next Sunday Gwen visited a new church. When she opened the bulletin, she read, *Wanted: Director at Alpha Alternative Pregnancy Center, part-time position in Hopkinsville, KY*. Hopkinsville was forty miles from Madisonville. Gwen knew this had to be God!

"Now, God," Gwen prayed, "you know this is my job." And it was. Not only was she hired, but the part-time director position paid the same as her full-time job.

Shortly after that, Gwen got married, and within three months she was pregnant. She found herself conflicted because of her desire to be home with her child and her desire to follow God's call to the pregnancy center. She and her husband, Brett, began to pray about what to do. One day she prayed, "God, you are the one who gave me the vision for a center in Madisonville and you are the one who gave me this baby. What am I supposed to do?"

Immediately, Gwen felt freedom from God to stay home with her child. She resigned as executive director of the Hopkinsville center. She was soon invited back to the ministry as a board member.

Gwen and Brett named their baby Hope (Gwen's middle name) and joyfully awaited her birth. But in Gwen's seventh month of pregnancy—September 1994—she began having contractions. An ultrasound revealed that Hope's lungs were not functioning properly; the excess amniotic fluid resulting from this condition was causing premature labor. Gwen's ob-gyn said there was a fifty-fifty chance that Hope would live. Hope was also in the breech position, and because of her fragility, the only way for her to survive birth would be by cesarean section.

Gwen remembers October 10, 1994, as probably the darkest day of her life up to that point. The ob-gyn called to tell her, "The fetus has trisomy 18, a genetic disorder incompatible with life." He said that delivery by cesarean was no longer an option, and he told Gwen to come to his office the next day. "We will induce labor and take care of this."

"No way!" Gwen replied. "We will come in tomorrow, but we will not 'take care of this'!"

That night was devastating. Gwen and Brett mourned and prayed. By the time Gwen met with the ob-gyn the next morning, she was having contractions and the baby had unexpectedly turned. She and Brett begged God for a miracle, but told him, "If you do not save Hope, we still trust you."

As the young couple waited for Hope to be born, they prayed and discussed what they would do if she did not survive. They decided to ask that any memorial donations be given to Alpha Alternative Pregnancy Center. Gwen hoped to use the funds to open a phone line that pregnant women in Madisonville could use to call the center in Hopkinsville for help.

The doctors prepared them for the possibilities that Hope would have deformities and would not be born alive. More than anything, Brett and Gwen wanted their daughter to live. But if she didn't, they hoped that her short life could bring hope to women in their community who were considering abortion.

Little Hope was born alive on October 11, 1994. She was three pounds, eleven ounces, and appeared beautiful and perfect. Gwen remembers, "We got to hold and love her for twenty minutes, then place her in God's arms forever."

During the dark time that followed, Gwen questioned God, searched Scripture, and tried to understand the death of her daughter. There were times when she couldn't even pray.

Meanwhile, about one thousand dollars was donated to Alpha Alternative in Hope's memory. The money was used to establish a Madisonville phone line, just as Gwen had envisioned.

But then God started revealing a larger plan. Someone offered an office building in Madisonville to be used as a pregnancy center. Someone else provided office furniture. Donations in Hope's memory continued to flow in as God multiplied the initial thousand dollars. Gwen became the executive director of Alpha once again, this time in charge of starting the satellite in Madisonville.

With Gwen as director, Madisonville's Door of Hope Pregnancy Center opened in September 1995. Gwen says, "To see all that happen—the fruit of Hope's short life—is astonishing to me! Even today, all these years later, I am astonished. We all pray for our children to be used for God's glory. But parents expect to hold their children, watch them grow, and then let them go to be a missionary or something. God had a different plan for Hope!"

Gwen and Brett had two more daughters, Hannah and Abby. Following the birth of her second daughter, Gwen resigned as director of the center to focus on raising her children. In the next four years, God blessed her with two sons, Jett and Robert.

Meanwhile, Gwen stayed involved with the center as a board member. Through this work, she learned of center clients who were grieving pregnancy loss. Gwen and her friend Teale Factor, who had lost two babies through miscarriage, wanted to provide Christ's hope to these clients. They developed a pregnancy-loss Bible study called *Threads of Hope, Pieces of Joy* and shared it with the Door of Hope Center.

But God had bigger plans. Requests began to pour in for copies of *Threads of Hope, Pieces of Joy*. The Bible study was offered for sale by Focus on the

Family, Elisabeth Elliot, and Loving and Caring. It is still available on Amazon. "We created it to help locally, but God has used it around the world to help globally," says Gwen with amazement.

People often thank Gwen for all she has done for their community. But Gwen knows that in her heartbroken state after Hope's birth and death, she couldn't do anything on her own. She says, "The Lord planted a seed in my heart to start a pregnancy center. Then he literally placed Hope in my body. He brought those two things together to accomplish his will for his glory. Hope's life taught me that if God can do so much with what the world would call an imperfect, twenty-minute life, what could he do with mine?"

Gwen recollects a particularly special memory: In 2003, when she was enrolling her son in preschool, a stranger asked if she was Gwen Kik with Door of Hope Pregnancy Center. The woman pointed to a three-year-old boy with a buzz haircut and said, "He is my grandson. I want to thank you because without the Door of Hope, we wouldn't have him."

Over the years Gwen watched that little buzz-cut guy grow into an incredible young man and a National Merit Scholar. He is just one of the thousands of babies born through Door of Hope in the last twenty-six years.

Gwen remains on the Door of Hope board of directors. The center continues to serve the Madisonville area, saving babies, loving their parents, and sharing the gospel. The book *Threads of Hope, Pieces of Joy* continues to minister to those suffering pregnancy loss. And Gwen continues to give God the glory.

"I wanted to save one baby, but God has saved many babies through the life of that one baby," she says. "And I wouldn't go back and change a thing."

LEADERSHIP INSIGHT

And we know that in all things God works for the good of those
who love him, who have been called according to his purpose.

—Romans 8:28

This verse is a life raft for those who have suffered a pregnancy loss. The Bible is clear that God can bring good even out of what the enemy intends for evil. Because God is good, there is a purpose in everything, even in suffering.

In Romans, Paul teaches that the ultimate purpose of suffering is hope—"and hope does not put us to shame" (Romans 5:5). Hope is what helps clients make decisions for life, and it is one of the greatest sources of comfort a leader has to offer to those who have experienced a pregnancy loss, whether a now-regretted abortion, a miscarriage, or infant death.

As a leader, you must help build a bridge for grieving clients to cross over to the giver of hope.

LET'S PRAY:

Father, thank you that in our suffering we learn to trust in you. Thank you for giving us hope and pouring your love into our hearts through the Holy Spirit. Our hope and the hope of our clients who are suffering is in you, and you never disappoint. Amen.

HOW DO YOU LIVE IT?

1. How would you explain the hope that is woven throughout Gwen's story?
2. Why is hope important to those suffering from a pregnancy loss?
3. How will Gwen's story help you lead in your pro-life calling?

5 | TRUTH
THE CANDY GIBBS STORY

Then you will know the truth, and the truth will set you free.

—John 8:32

When Candy Gibbs learned that her pregnancy test was positive, she realized her world was about to be turned upside down.

She also knew that she would not get an abortion. Her dad was a youth pastor, and their family was committed to walking in truth—including the truth that every human life is precious.

Growing up, Candy was shy and insecure; she longed desperately to fit in. In her junior year of high school she became a cheerleader, and she fell for a good-looking, popular young man. She was flattered by his attention and soon infatuated. Against her parents' rules, she began dating him—sneaking around, lying, making one compromise after another, and ignoring the truth of the Christian values that had always guided her life.

It wasn't long before the relationship turned sexual, and everything changed. Candy started to wonder if her boyfriend was ready to move on from her now that they had become sexually intimate. However, she thought she had to stay with him. She knew that sex was just for marriage, and she rationalized that if they stayed together, he would remain the only person she had slept with. The relationship quickly became dysfunctional, even physically abusive.

During her senior year of high school, Candy missed a period. She went to a nearby location of Care Net Centers of Amarillo (now Hope Choice Pregnancy Centers and Mentoring Programs) where her fears were confirmed: she was pregnant. When she told her boyfriend, his response was, "I am sorry this happened. Do whatever you want, but I'm out of it."

Devastated, she had to tell her dad that not only had she been dating this boy behind his back, but she was pregnant. Emotions ran high as the family processed the news. Finally, they reached a decision: Candy had to have an abortion.

A week later, Candy's dad took her to a place she had never expected to be—an abortion clinic. Although the waiting room was full, Candy felt alone. Candy said that her dad later told her he judged the other women waiting for abortions, wondering, "How can you people do this?" But he thought Candy's situation was an exception.

After Candy's abortion, she and her family went into an emotional and spiritual tailspin. Candy began to experience such overwhelming emotional pain, turmoil, and hopelessness that she shut down her emotions completely. Her life no longer felt worth living.

Candy's parents questioned themselves and each other for not being more aware of their daughter's needs and the behavior that led to her pregnancy. Most of all, they questioned if the abortion of Candy's baby was really the right choice. Candy's parents almost divorced as a result of this extremely difficult time.

Two years after the abortion, Candy was still struggling. Feeling hopeless, she remembered the love and acceptance she had experienced at the pregnancy center where she had gone for her pregnancy test. Desperately hoping for help, she contacted the center and learned that they offered a Bible study for abortion recovery. Candy didn't think this would help her, but she signed up for the study anyway.

During the Bible study, Candy was able to face the truth about the choices she had made—especially the painful truth about her choice to end the life of her baby. "The truth I found was that although my abortion was irreversible, it was forgivable," Candy says.

Embracing that truth and accepting God's love and forgiveness set her free. "It changed the trajectory of my life," she says. "Through that course, I was able to give my daughter a name: Jessica." For the first time in two years, Candy found the strength and support she needed to receive God's forgiveness and then forgive herself.

Once Candy experienced that freedom, she knew she was called to help others walk in the truth, too. She became a volunteer at the pregnancy center, then served on their abstinence team, and later became a secretary and then a branch director. In 2002, the board asked her to become executive director of the Care Net Pregnancy Centers of Amarillo. She says, "It is the most beautiful thing to me that God has allowed me to work in this ministry that was a lifesaver and a blessing in my own life."

Now a mom of three adult children, Candy continues to lead this thriving community pregnancy center ministry, which serves about thirteen hundred people a month in its four offices. In 2000, the center began offering mentoring programs using curricula written by Candy. Today, seven mentoring programs are provided by a fifty-person speaking team.

Two of the programs are in public schools, enabling the team to interact with twenty-two thousand students each month of the school year. Candy says, "It is my prayer that we can impact their lives before they find themselves in that place where my family found ourselves many years ago."

When she launched the mentoring programs, Candy's heart was to help teen girls. The first program was a Bible-based study for high school girls called Pearls. "Just to see young ladies impacted by the Word of God and by the truth about who they are, who he has called them to be, and how that can change the way they see themselves is amazing!" exclaims Candy. "Although I was a pastor's daughter, I didn't know my worth. Now I get to empower young women to thrive in the same areas where I struggled."

One of the school mentoring programs is a character development program for kindergarten through high school. There is also a leadership development program for middle school and high school students.

"The one thing a pro-life leader has to do is to tell the truth," says Candy. "As a leader, you have to be comfortable standing on the side of God's Word. No matter what the culture does, or if someone you love makes a sinful decision, God's Word is still truth.

"As a leader, you love people while still standing on the side of truth."

As a national speaker on pro-life leadership, Candy encourages leaders who might be struggling: "Don't quit! Every leader goes through times when they feel like they aren't equipped for their mission. But keep going! We need to see those in front of us carrying the flag—and God will bless your persistence."

LEADERSHIP INSIGHT

Instead, speaking the truth in love, we will grow to become in every respect the mature body of him who is the head, that is, Christ.

—Ephesians 4:15

At one time the Peace Corps had the slogan, *The toughest job you'll ever love.* Isn't that an apt description for pro-life ministry, too? As Candy says, it is hard work; we may feel ill equipped, the days are sometimes long, and it is emotionally costly.

But at the same time, it is a work of love. Through sharing the truth of God's generous love, we get to see clients set free in Christ Jesus!

Do not give up. Keep pursuing the mission God has called you to through Christ Jesus. In doing so, you are following the one who is the way, the truth, and the life.

Leaders love people unconditionally and share God's truth unashamedly. You must persistently stand on truth to keep the movement for life advancing to the glory of God.

LET'S PRAY:

Thank you, Father, for calling us to demonstrate your love by speaking the truth with compassion to those who are making pregnancy decisions. We know it's a privilege to speak into these desperate moments in our clients' lives. Fill us with the knowledge of your will, that we may live worthy of your calling and please you in every way. Strengthen us with all power so that we may endure through any difficulty. In the mighty name of Jesus, to the glory of God, amen.

HOW DO YOU LIVE IT?

1. Where do you see the characteristic of truth in Candy's life?

2. What are the reasons why some laborers do not persist in pro-life ministry?

3. How can Candy's encouragement to stand on the side of truth help you persist in your pro-life calling?

6 | LOVING & CARING
THE ANNE PIERSON STORY

If God has given you leadership ability, take the responsibility seriously. And if you have a gift for showing kindness to others, do it gladly. Don't just pretend to love others. Really love them. Hate what is wrong. Hold tightly to what is good.

—Romans 12:8–9 (NLT)

Loving and caring: these words bring Anne Pierson to mind. Not only do they describe Anne and the motivation of her pro-life work, they also identify the organization she cofounded.

While Anne and her husband, Jim, were in youth ministry in Washington, DC, their lives were first touched by a young woman experiencing an unplanned pregnancy. They met a pregnant college student who had been rejected by her parents and had nowhere to live.

As a freshman, this young woman and two of her friends had attended a campus party together, and all three had become pregnant that night. Together, the three girls went to have abortions. Although her two friends each got an abortion, the young woman could not go through with it. Instead, she called her parents for help. Angrily they refused to allow her to come home, and they stopped paying for her college education.

When the young woman met Anne and Jim, she was desperate.

The pro-life movement had not yet begun. In those early days, homes for pregnant, unwed women were hidden away, and no pregnancy centers existed. But Anne and Jim already had a heart to love and care for women and their unborn babies. They invited the college student into their already overcrowded three-bedroom home, where they lived with their two children and Anne's grandfather.

While caring for this young woman, the couple discovered that there were hundreds of women in their community who were facing unplanned pregnancies. "All of a sudden, this world opened up to me that I didn't know existed," Anne recalls.

In 1973, Anne and Jim found an opportunity to make a difference for women in this situation. A pastor in Pennsylvania asked them to help start a home for unwed mothers. They moved to Pennsylvania, where they bought an old farmhouse from an elderly couple. The wife, who was dying, told them that she and her husband had been praying for their home to be used to help young people. Jim and Anne called their maternity home "House of His Creation," and in the course of their time there, they loved and cared for over a hundred young women.

Meanwhile, evangelical leaders Francis Schaeffer, C. Everett Koop, and Harold O. J. and Grace Brown met in Billy Graham's home in 1975 to discuss ideas for reversing *Roe v. Wade*. The group established the Christian Action Council (CAC) to educate the public and lobby Congress.

"One day," Anne recounts, "we got a call telling us that President Reagan was going to mention us and our work in a speech. He didn't refer to us by name, but word got out that he was talking about us." People from all over began contacting the Piersons for help with starting pro-life ministries.

Then, the president himself called Anne and Jim and a group of other pioneer pro-life workers together to brainstorm pro-life strategies.

The pro-life movement had begun!

CAC contacted Anne and Jim, too. The group had developed a model for pregnancy resource centers, and they invited Anne and Jim to join in their mission of establishing and equipping pregnancy centers to empower women in making life-affirming decisions. Consequently, Anne developed CAC's first center operations manual. CAC opened its first pregnancy center—in Baltimore, Maryland—in 1980. In 1999, CAC adopted the name Care Net.

The pregnancy center movement had begun!

Meanwhile, Jim and Anne maintained their focus on maternity homes. Within ten years they established two homes, along with a facility for mothers who had chosen adoption for their children and an extended family living program for women parenting their children.

Seeing the need to help the women make better choices for themselves and their babies, Anne began to write curricula. One of her most popular books, *My Baby and Me*, sold over 460,000 copies. Anne was also in much demand as a speaker at pro-life events.

Jim and Anne had become a sought-after resource for materials and guidance. In 1984, they turned the maternity home operations over to others and established Loving and Caring, a national and international ministry that provided resources and assistance to the pro-life community.

Jim went home to be with Jesus in 2012. Anne continued providing resources through Loving and Caring for eight more years. Several years ago, she authored *Love's Open Door*, an account of her ministry journey with Jim. She also shared insights given to her by the Lord in a blog on the Loving and Caring website.

Many of the pro-life workers Anne advises call her "the grandmother of the pro-life movement." And that she is!

"I don't think of myself as a leader," Anne reflects. "I've never been about building a giant ministry. I like to think that I'm just a person that, when people meet me, they see the heart of God, are encouraged to believe in themselves, and hear God's heart for them and his call on their lives—and that they are inspired and have the courage to make a difference for him."

In 2020, after nearly fifty years, Anne retired from public ministry. But her personal ministry to everyone she meets continues. Presently serving on the board of Water Street Mission in Lancaster, Pennsylvania, she devotes her time to leading Bible studies for the women at the mission. Anne is committed to showing people they are loved. She keeps praying and walking through the doors God opens.

"Pro-life workers need to know that their work really matters and makes an impact," she says. "My message is to stop striving. Jesus never strived. In obedience to God, he just loved all those God gave him—even unto death. My greatest desire is that we be like Jesus and just keep obeying God, loving and caring for those he gives us and trusting him for the results."

LEADERSHIP INSIGHT

He renews my strength. He guides me along right paths,
bringing honor to his name.

—Psalm 23:3 (NLT)

Ralph Waldo Emerson is often quoted as saying, "Do not go where the path may lead, go instead where there is no path and leave a trail."

God gave Anne Pierson courage to walk where there was no pro-life path and the ability to love and care for others along the way. The materials she authored blazed a trail for others to follow. It is not an exaggeration to say that nearly everyone in compassionate pro-life ministry in North America has been touched, directly or indirectly, by Anne's ministry.

People who spend even a few moments with Anne report feeling seen. Just by loving and caring, she has inspired and equipped generations to carry on her pro-life work.

> Leaders must steward the abilities God has given them. The best leaders inspire, love, and care for others, never using or manipulating them.

LET'S PRAY:

Father, we thank you for your gift of leadership. Teach us to take that responsibility seriously as we serve you in pro-life work. Help us use your gifts to show love and care to those who are hurting. May we go where you call us. Show us how to leave a well-marked trail that others may follow. Amen.

HOW DO YOU LIVE IT?

1. What are some of the ways Anne loved and cared for those God placed in her path?

2. How did Anne blaze a trail for others to follow?

3. In what ways has God equipped you to show love and to care for those you lead?

The voice of the Lord is powerful; the voice of the Lord is majestic.
—Psalm 29:4 (NLT)

One encounter with God changed the direction of Jim Sprague's life.

It was the summer of 1980, and Jim was about to attend Michigan State University. He had turned his back on his Christian upbringing and, in his own words, was attending college "to self-indulge." He says, "If they wanted to give me a degree, that would be fine, but that certainly wasn't why I was going."

That summer, Jim's good friend and mentor, Dwight, drowned in a boating accident. Dwight was a strong Christian. He didn't necessarily agree with Jim's lifestyle, but he was the only Christian Jim knew who didn't make him feel judged. Jim was devastated when his beloved friend died.

As a pallbearer sitting in the front row at Dwight's funeral, Jim raged silently at God: "You took the wrong guy. You should have taken me. You know I am not living a life pleasing to you, but Dwight was. I don't understand you! Why did you take him?"

Jim then sensed the presence of the Almighty God. He felt the warmth of God's hand on his shoulder as he whispered in Jim's ear, "Jim, it is not too late for you."

In that divine encounter, Jim knew he was being given a chance to turn his life around. By faith, he took the bold step of enrolling in Grand Rapids Baptist College (now Cornerstone University) instead of attending MSU.

In December of that year, before starting college, Jim attended a Christian music concert in Grand Rapids. In the crowd of people, Jim happened to run into Jack, who had been Dwight's coworker. Jack now worked for a ministry that helped troubled young men, and he asked Jim to come work for him as a mentor. Jim says, "I look back now and think, *What irony!* I was a troubled young man myself." However, Jim accepted the position. He realizes now that God was directing his path, because at the ministry he met his wife, Jody.

Jim and Jody were married in 1985, the same year that their church launched the Pregnancy Resource Center of Grand Rapids. The young couple's hearts were profoundly touched by the pro-life cause. Jody joined the first volunteer training class and served at the center for many years. She eventually joined the board of directors.

For the first nine years of their marriage, Jim and Jody tried to get pregnant, but were heartbroken month after month. The doctors were baffled by their inability to conceive. The couple considered adoption but could not give up their dream to have biological children.

Then Jim heard a sermon on the Apostle Paul's adoption doctrine. Paul wrote that we are all adopted into God's family—and that adoption secures us the same inheritance as that of his biological son, Jesus.

During that sermon, Jim again sensed the tangible presence of the Almighty God. Again he felt the warmth of God's hand on his shoulder and heard God's whisper in his ear: "Jim, you need to listen to this." Jim knew then that adoption was God's will for their family.

By faith, Jim and Jody began the process of qualifying for foster care and adoption. They received a home license and prepared to welcome a child.

Meanwhile, Susan became pregnant at age sixteen, but told no one. When she began to have abdominal pain, her parents—thinking Susan had appendicitis—rushed her to the hospital. After an examination, the doctor broke the news to Susan's parents that she was pregnant and in labor. On March 17, 1994, Susan delivered a baby boy. She decided to place her child for adoption.

The very next day, Jim and Jody learned about their son Jacob's birth and held him for the first time. Suddenly they were parents.

Jim and Jody's family continued to grow through adoption. In January 2000, their daughter Madison was born, and their son Kevin was born three years later. "Thankfully," Jim says, "the birth mothers of our children did not choose abortion, but chose life and adoption. For me that makes the work we do at the PRC personal, significant, and extremely profound."

God orchestrated several events that brought Jim firmly into pro-life ministry. In 2001, Jim was job hunting—and Grand Rapids PRC was searching for a new CEO. At that time, through the adoption of his children, Jim felt compelled to become more personally involved in protecting unborn lives. He applied for the CEO position and was hired in April 2001.

Now in his twentieth year as CEO, Jim's current passion is to share with other centers the effective three-pillar model that God has been developing at the PRC.

The first pillar is this: centers exist to serve the Bride of Christ. Jim is strongly motivated by the abortions that happen in churchgoing families. He says with sadness, "These are our kids!" Jim's desire is to make abortion unthinkable in the church—this is why he is extremely passionate about partnering with Care Net to equip people of faith to disciple young couples who are making pregnancy decisions.

Pillar number two is that, even while being culturally relevant, centers must remain faithful to their pro-abundant-life gospel message.

The last pillar, pursuing excellence, is drawn from Isaiah 54:2: "Stretch your tent curtains . . . strengthen your stakes." Centers must stretch and grow to meet future needs. Jim encourages them to "strengthen their stakes" by using the best technology and training to work with excellence, honoring God.

God's presence—his touch and his whisper—is woven into the fabric of Jim Sprague's story. Jim says, "My story is one of God-encounters as he redirected my life." And God has continued to direct Jim's successful pro-life work for two decades.

As Jim reflects on those years, he says (quoting Psalm 90:17), "When I started at the PRC, I had no inkling that our work would become a major political issue, and more important and exciting than ever. I see God stirring the hearts of pro-life people as never before. I pray that 'the favor of the Lord our God will rest on all of us and establish the work of our hands for us' for his glory."

LEADERSHIP INSIGHT

You see that his faith and his actions were working together,
and his faith was made complete by what he did.

—James 2:22

In those key moments when God spoke to him, Jim responded by faith and with actions. His faith was made complete by what he did. Jim's actions led him on a path of leadership and fruitful ministry.

Scripture tells us that faith without action is dead. We know that without faith, it is impossible to please God. In the same way, it is impossible to be a leader for life without faith—faith completed by actions.

Remember that you walk by faith and not by sight, and that leaders live by faith, serve by faith, and lead by faith. Your faith will be made complete by your actions.

LET'S PRAY:

God, we pray that you will enable pro-life leaders to live lives worthy of your calling. Give us the power and faith to accomplish all the things you have called us to do. Lord Jesus Christ and God our Father, would you encourage the hearts of leaders and strengthen us in every good deed and word? In Jesus' name, amen.

HOW DO YOU LIVE IT?

1. How did faith make a difference in Jim's life?
2. How did actions make Jim's faith complete?
3. Share why both faith and action are important in leadership.

8 | HUMILITY
THE MARY LEQUIEU STORY

But the plans of the Lord stand firm forever, the purposes of his heart through all generations.

—Psalm 33:11

"The whole pro-life connection began for me before I was born," Mary LeQuieu says. "In Scripture it says God had plans for us before the beginning of the world. I certainly see that in my life."

She goes on, her voice reflective: "In 1951, my parents were expecting their second child—me. They were excited about having another baby." But five weeks into the pregnancy, Mary's mother began to bleed. Her doctor was unavailable during the emergency, but his partner determined she was losing the baby. If her baby survived, he said, it would be mentally and physically impaired. His solution was to give her "medicine" to terminate the pregnancy.

When the primary doctor was told about his partner's attempt to end the pregnancy, he gave Mary's mother an injection of progesterone to reverse the abortion. "That doctor saved my life," says Mary. "God had his hand on me before I was born, before the beginning of the world."

When Mary was born, she functioned perfectly. She was most likely one of the first babies to have her life saved from an abortion by progesterone, a protocol now known as abortion pill reversal.

Mary was raised in a Christian home. However, as a child she was sexually assaulted twice by a houseguest. She believes that this traumatic experience distorted her perspective on sexuality and on her own self-worth, leading to unwise sexual activity in college. In spite of those experiences, Mary remembers that she deeply wanted God's approval and thought that serving those with less would please him. So, when she was in college, she went on a mission trip to South America.

While there she became intimately involved with a young pastor. Suspecting that she was pregnant, he told her to get rid of "it." She was shocked, and returned home rejected and hurt.

Back home, Mary went to her doctor, who confirmed her pregnancy. When the doctor asked if she wanted to be pregnant, Mary answered no. The doctor responded that she "didn't do that kind of thing." It was 1973, two months after the *Roe v. Wade* decision, and Mary didn't even know what abortion was or what her doctor meant. Regardless, the doctor gave her the address for an abortion clinic.

At the clinic, Mary tried to ask about maternity homes. But the doctor became angry with her. When Mary asked what her baby looked like, he told her it looked like a pre-evolutionary fish. He leaned over her and said angrily, "Stop wasting my time! Sign the papers!"

Fearfully and obediently, Mary signed the papers consenting to an abortion, and the doctor started the abortion process that day.

The next day, during the abortion procedure, Mary had an allergic reaction to Demerol and nearly died. She recovered because of the hospital staff's quick treatment of her symptoms. "They saved my life, but they didn't save my child's life," she laments.

For about two weeks, Mary felt relief. But that relief didn't last. Soon she was caught in a cycle of regret. For months Mary felt listless and depressed, then angry. Nearly overwhelmed with guilt, she began to try to replace the baby she lost, moving from sexual encounter to sexual encounter. Today, Mary would recognize these as symptoms of after-abortion regret. But at the time, the turmoil inside threatened to consume her.

Mary began to search for ways to relieve her pain. She attended Moody Bible Institute, where she saturated herself in Scripture and came to understand that Christ takes away sin and forgives. But she was still hurting.

Soon after leaving Moody, Mary found the courage to tell a few trusted friends about her abortion and her struggles since. One of her friends encouraged her to release her child and her pain to God by creating a "feelings box."

In a symbolic ceremony of releasing, Mary placed a letter she had written to her unborn child and some baby items in a small box. With her friend, she buried the box in her backyard. Through this simple act, Mary was finally able to release her pain and her child to God.

Mary got married in 1978, and she became pregnant right away. Hearing her baby's heartbeat during an ultrasound, she realized that this baby was the same age as the one she had aborted. Painful memories of the abortion flooded back, and unbelievable rage welled up in her toward the doctor who took her first child. She began to hate and distrust all doctors. Throughout her pregnancy, Mary grieved the loss of her first baby again.

Her grief propelled her into action to try to help other women facing unplanned pregnancies. Mary's church supported the Care Net Pregnancy Center of Albuquerque, where her sister-in-law volunteered and another church friend was the executive director. When the position of center services director opened up, Mary applied and was hired.

The center had sought someone to fill the position for six months, but no one had applied in all that time except Mary. After she was hired, the center was then flooded with resumes. Mary believes that God miraculously led her to the center and to that specific job at exactly the right time.

Because Mary had had an abortion, she was asked to join the center's postabortion recovery Bible study. That's when she discovered that, by leading her to the center, God had given her the opportunity not only to help other women but to find complete healing herself. Although she had received Christ in her heart nearly twenty years before, she had never felt that she deserved God's love. Through the Bible study, she was able to accept God's unconditional love. Finally, Mary felt forgiven and set free.

Mary calls this "the unfair exchange": God took her sin and exchanged it for his righteousness. She says, "He not only takes our sin and gives us salvation, he also takes all the junk in our life, redeems it, and uses it for his glory. To me it is astounding that he would do that!"

Mary says she "loved, loved, loved being a center services director and being in the client room, where God takes your words and explodes them into someone's heart where they are desperately needed." She calls the client room "holy ground."

Under Mary's leadership, together with John Douglas, the executive director, the ministry grew from one to four centers. To accommodate all God was doing, the board restructured in 2008, making John the development director and Mary the executive director.

In those early years as executive director, Mary felt like she was in over her head. When people would tell her that she was doing a great job, Mary would say, "It's a team of staff, volunteers, donors, and, most of all, God that is doing a great job!"

"God does amazing things!" Mary says. When the center was given an old Winnebago with bad brakes and a leaking engine, Mary and her team used it to provide services on one university campus and five community college campuses. Mary says, "God provided the doors of opportunity and we just walked through them."

Soon God opened a door to collaboration with a local hospital. The hospital's physicians developed a policy ending elective abortions and were further living out their pro-life convictions by providing support to women facing unplanned pregnancies. The hospital hired a pregnancy center liaison and implemented a program to fast-track pregnancy center clients to medical care and other benefits. Through Mary's leadership, the hospital became a strong partner: the center helping hospital patients with pregnancy support, and the center's clients receiving medical care through the hospital.

Later, the hospital contributed $50,000 toward the purchase of a medical vehicle for the center. The center began to take the vehicle—fully equipped with an ultrasound machine and a private meeting place—to nearby university and community college campuses.

And that was just the beginning. Mary and her team also began setting up the medical vehicle near a New Mexico clinic that is infamous for terminating even full-term pregnancies. In partnership with Sidewalk Advocates for Life, a national organization that shares the compassionate attitude of the center, they provide ultrasounds and offer hope and help to women seeking abortions.

Mary recounts one of her most memorable experiences at this abortion clinic. A mother had gone into the clinic for a scheduled abortion, and the baby's father, who was waiting outside, was told that free ultrasounds were available. After the mother checked in at the clinic, she came back outside for a smoke break, already wearing her medical ID bracelet—and her boyfriend persuaded her to have an ultrasound. When they saw the amazing image of their baby and learned about their options and the support available to them, they decided not to go through with the abortion. "I'll never forget," Mary laughingly says, "that young mother immediately yanked the medical ID bracelet off her arm, threw it in the trash, and went home."

The medical vehicle also travels to rural community pregnancy centers that are unable to offer medical services. Mary relates, "God's fingerprints are clearly all over this traveling medical service, promoting life across New Mexico. He truly envisioned this."

In 2020, Mary retired from Care Net Pregnancy Centers of Albuquerque. Even now, talking about how God has grown her as a leader, she thinks first of her team. "As I look back, what we did seems impossible. And it would be, were it not for the people God called to the work with me. They have such passion for serving clients—and for doing so with excellence." According to Mary, the team stretches beyond the pregnancy center's staff and volunteers. She also gratefully credits donors, prayer partners, and Care Net's training, curriculum, and resources. "Even after more than eighteen years of ministry, I'm so blessed to be equipped and supported by my Care Net family."

"God takes people who are willing and available and he does amazing things!" Mary declares. "All you need to do is depend on him. God's heart is for this ministry, and he provides."

LEADERSHIP INSIGHT

He has shown you, O mortal, what is good. And what does the Lord require of you? To act justly and to love mercy and to walk humbly with your God.

—Micah 6:8

Micah 6:8 describes Mary's life and leadership—she walks humbly with her God. She takes no credit for all the work she does. Rather, she gives all the credit to God and to the team that he has brought to her.

This verse could also be seen as the job description for all pro-life leaders. Leaders must always depend on the power of God and serve him. He requires all leaders to act justly, love mercy, and walk humbly with him. Depend on him—he will do amazing things!

As you walk humbly with God, he will build a team to do the work with you and he will fully equip you for leadership.

LET'S PRAY:

Father, we humbly trust in you with all our hearts. We do not lean on our own understanding. Thank you, Lord, that you walk with us, meet all our needs, and make us worthy of your calling, for the good of the unborn, for their families, and for your glory. Amen.

HOW DO YOU LIVE IT?

1. How do you see humility in Mary's story?

2. What Scripture passage speaks to you personally about humility?

3. How can that Scripture passage help you in your pro-life leadership?

9 | COMPASSION
THE YVONNE WILLIAMS STORY

Praise be to the God and Father of our Lord Jesus Christ, the Father of compassion and the God of all comfort, who comforts us in all our troubles, so that we can comfort those in any trouble with the comfort we ourselves receive from God.

—2 Corinthians 1:3–4

"On my Colorado college campus in 1969, I was one of the leaders of the pack," Yvonne Williams recalls. She and her boyfriend, Warren, had each been raised in church, but had left their faith when they went to college. "We were all in the bar and drug scene. A lot of my friends attended the same parties I did. We hung out at the same places. When one of them would get pregnant, they would come to me because Warren and I would take them to Mexico for an abortion. We believed we were being compassionate, helping and comforting women in trouble."

After helping their friends obtain abortions for some time, Yvonne and Warren began to notice the heartache and tragedy that followed. These women wept for their lost children. They dropped out or flunked out of college. They would abuse alcohol and drugs. Yvonne and Warren became so distressed by these outcomes that they quit facilitating the Mexico abortions altogether.

"Then, in 1970, it was my turn!" Yvonne says. "I was pregnant! I went to a doctor for an abortion. He gave me some pills to end the pregnancy, but they didn't work. Praise God, my child lived!"

When Yvonne told Warren she was pregnant, they decided they really wanted this baby. They married and had a beautiful baby girl. Wanting to be the best parents they could be for their daughter, they went back to church when she was about three months old and committed their lives to Christ.

Then, on a cold day in January 1973, the Supreme Court made the tragic *Roe v. Wade* decision. Having seen firsthand the pain of abortion, Yvonne and

Warren knew this decision could only hurt women.

Warren wanted them to start a ministry giving women an alternative to abortion, but with a small child to care for, the timing was wrong for Yvonne. So in June 1974, Warren, with the help of a few volunteers, started a "crisis hotline" in Boulder, answering calls from women making pregnancy decisions.

One day, Yvonne visited the center to see what it was all about. She recounts, "The phone rang and a woman started talking to Warren about her menstrual cycle. He turned beet red and handed the phone to me." So, Yvonne began volunteering for the hotline.

In 1975, the ministry began operating as a pregnancy center, Birthright of Boulder, and Yvonne became the executive director. "Now, well over forty years later, I am still answering the phone," Yvonne says. "I am still working in my God-given calling to help women in making life decisions."

In those early years, pregnancy centers were loosely organized. Yvonne remembers center directors discovering best practices as they went along because there were no training manuals. Directors talked to other directors— if one found an approach that worked at their center, others would try it at their centers.

At first, pregnancy centers were thought of as a short-term solution. Pro-life workers believed that in a few years America would come to its senses, and *Roe v. Wade* and *Doe v. Bolton* would be overturned. They were certain that all women needed to carry their babies to term was accurate information.

At the time, ultrasound was revealing more and more about the life of children in the womb. Yvonne recalls an old *Life* magazine cover from 1965, featuring an image of a preborn baby. America had been stunned by it, and she and Warren used it to educate clients about fetal development. Still abortion stayed legal. Eventually, pro-life workers realized that pregnancy centers would be needed long-term to empower women and men to choose life.

For Warren and Yvonne, a revolutionary realization occurred when they were holding an abortion recovery meeting for women in a church basement. During the meeting, Warren came upon a janitor sitting on the floor of the supply room, weeping. "What happened to you, man?" Warren asked. "Did you get hurt?"

"I have been listening to the meeting," the janitor replied. "I paid to abort my children. I participated in the deaths of my own children!"

That stunning revelation led Warren in 1978 to initiate postabortion care for men. Throughout his lifetime of serving men who have been hurt by abortion, Warren has written Bible studies and developed training manuals for men's ministry.

As Yvonne says of her and Warren's work, "It is really *our* story, embracing both sides of the life issue—women and men."

In 1988, Birthright of Boulder affiliated with the CAC (now Care Net) as the Boulder Pregnancy Center. Looking back, Yvonne feels privileged to have helped implement significant changes in the pregnancy center movement: the addition of ultrasound exams, improved pregnancy tests, abortion recovery support groups and Bible studies, training and operational manuals, and more.

Because of her own college experience, bringing life-affirming ministry to college campuses is especially close to Yvonne's heart. She helped start the nation's first pregnancy center on a college campus in 1992, when she established a satellite of the Boulder Pregnancy Center at the University of Colorado Boulder. She has also worked with Care Net in the development of a handbook to enable other pregnancy centers to create effective campus ministries.

In 1999, after twenty-five years of directing the pregnancy center in Boulder, Yvonne began working with Care Net as a consultant and center services specialist, helping hundreds of pregnancy centers be more effective.

She and Warren still make their home in Boulder. One of the greatest blessings Yvonne has received from her long-term investment in one community is the opportunity to meet previous clients. It isn't rare for her to encounter someone in the community only to hear them say, "You helped me long ago, and I would like you to meet someone." That someone is always a child saved from abortion. Yvonne has watched some of these children grow up, marry, and have children of their own—a reminder of the long-term impact of pregnancy centers.

After Yvonne's departure, the Boulder Pregnancy Center merged with the Roman Catholic archdiocese and relocated. For three years, Boulder had no pregnancy center—but there were still unplanned pregnancies. Yvonne couldn't let go of the thought that God was calling her to help meet the need. With the support of Care Net and Focus on the Family, she did exactly that. Together with other community members, she established a new Boulder center in 2019, where she serves on the board. That center is now a Care Net affiliate.

Yvonne is still the same compassionate woman who tried to help pregnant students when she was in college. When her eyes were opened to the reality of the baby in the womb and the pain abortion causes, her compassion guided her into forty-plus years of serving in pro-life ministry. Today, the face of her precious daughter that she almost aborted and the faces of her beautiful grandchildren inspire her as she continues to serve in Boulder and across the nation.

LEADERSHIP INSIGHT

Therefore, as God's chosen people, holy and dearly loved, clothe yourselves with compassion, kindness, humility, gentleness and patience.

—Colossians 3:12

Yvonne Williams' heart of compassion has led her to a lifetime of comforting those who are hurting due to an unplanned pregnancy. Her heart of Godlike compassion continues to be expressed as she helps equip centers to comfort, empower, and support families to choose life for their unborn.

Like Yvonne, leaders need to understand how the Father of compassion has comforted them so that they can comfort others. To paraphrase Colossians 3:12, "Therefore, as God's chosen leaders for life, holy and dearly loved, clothe yourselves with compassion and express that compassion in kindness, humility, gentleness, and patience."

As a leader, you are called to pay forward with compassion the comfort given to you by the Father of compassion and the God of all comfort.

LET'S PRAY:

Father of compassion, God of all comfort, we praise and thank you for comforting us in all our troubles. Fill our hearts and our lives with your compassion that we may comfort others in their troubles. As leaders for life, may we be clothed with compassion, expressed in kindness, humility, gentleness, and patience—comforting those who are hurting. So be it in Jesus' name.

HOW DO YOU LIVE IT?

1. How did Yvonne experience God's compassion?

2. In what ways is Yvonne clothed with compassion?

3. Why is compassion a valuable characteristic for you as you lead a life-affirming ministry?

10 | SERVANT LEADERSHIP
THE CINDY HOPKINS STORY

Not so with you. Instead, whoever wants to become great among you must be your servant.

—Matthew 20:26

"My first personal encounter with someone seeking an abortion rocked my world," Cindy Hopkins reflects. Cindy was a young mother herself when a friend shared that she planned to have an abortion.

Cindy was passionately pro-life. She and her husband, Paul, had just had their second child, and she couldn't imagine a woman aborting her own baby. And, as a Christian, she knew that God was against abortion.

But she didn't know how to tell her friend that abortion was wrong without sounding judgmental. Cindy remembers saying things like "That's sin," "That's murder," "Why would you do that?" and "What are you thinking?" She couldn't understand why another Christian would make this choice.

Though Cindy offered her home and her help, her friend did choose abortion. Cindy was devastated. "The whole experience just bowled me over. I never wanted to go through that again—ever!"

Years earlier, Cindy had struggled with the question of what she should do with her life. After high school, she had tried studying nursing in college. When she failed her first chemistry test, she walked out of the classroom, drove off campus, and decided never to go back.

Not sure what was next, Cindy began seeking God's guidance. "Lord, where am I supposed to be?" she prayed. "What am I supposed to be doing? And who am I?"

Cindy eventually married and settled into a full-time job as a real estate appraiser in her home state of California. But then God led her and her husband, Paul, to a job opportunity near the college town of Ogden, Utah.

Now twenty-four years old, Cindy began to think about college again. With Paul's encouragement, she enrolled and studied business administration with an emphasis in marketing—not because she had clear plans for her future, but because she sensed God had her on a path that she didn't fully understand.

When she graduated at the top of her class, she was two months pregnant with her first child. Excited to raise a family, Cindy became a full-time homemaker. And she wondered, "Lord, what was that college journey all about?"

Cindy had two more babies and loved caring for her family. Focused on growing in the Lord, she went to Bible studies and got to know Jesus better. After all those years of questioning, Cindy knew she was right where God wanted her; yet she still wondered if there was more that God wanted her to do.

In 1990, she learned that a pregnancy center had just opened in her community. She wondered if this was where God was calling her.

Her friend's abortion years earlier still weighed on her. "I thought I could just go down there and tell people to stop it," she laughs. "My friend wouldn't listen to me, but these people would." And so she did "go down there" to the pregnancy center—but what God had in mind was far beyond what she had imagined.

Through the Care Net training she received at the center, Cindy realized that this place was exactly where God wanted her, but not to lecture and shame women away from abortion. Instead, she discovered the impact of sharing the truth with compassion so clients could find hope for their futures. God showed Cindy that facts can be compelling, but without a hefty dose of love, truth is just a clanging cymbal.

After volunteering and serving as a board member for four years, Cindy joined the center staff. Later, when the executive director resigned, the board asked her to fill the role. She hesitated in accepting the offer, thinking leadership of this kind was too far beyond her. That night, with Paul, she prayed that God would show her what to do.

When she woke up the next morning, she knew she was supposed to say yes.

She felt confident and capable. God had told her that he would show her how to lead . . . his way!

As Cindy began her leadership role at the center, she soon realized with amazement that she was using her business administration degree. She remembers thinking, "OK, God, you knew what you wanted me to do and you were preparing me. I was just walking blindly down the road trying to figure it out, and you were doing all of this behind the scenes." Cindy says now, "It was like a lightbulb went on and I could see his plan so clearly. Leadership was my sweet spot and God knew it all along."

In 2004, Cindy and Paul relocated to Virginia for Paul to accept a job with Lockheed-Martin. Excited to live near Care Net's national office (Cindy says tongue-in-cheek that she was a "Care Net groupie"), she immediately sent in her resume, but there were no openings at the time. She also sent resumes to local pregnancy centers. When she was hired as the director of outreach at Metro Women's Care Center, she was able to use her marketing education to reach people at risk for abortion. She also had the opportunity to coach potential clients on the phone and discovered that she loved it. This planted the seeds in her heart for a future ministry now known as Pregnancy Decision Line.

As God had planned all along, Cindy is now part of the leadership team at Care Net, where she serves as vice president of center services and client care. She celebrated fourteen years of service with Care Net in 2020. During this time, her department has grown from a staff of one to a team of nineteen.

In 2010, God opened the door for Cindy to get a master's degree in organizational leadership from Regent University. "I learned that the best leaders are the ones who lead like Jesus."

The bedrock of Cindy's leadership is love and trust for every member of her team. She cares about them as people, not just their productivity at work. She prays with and for her team, encourages and empowers them, has difficult conversations with them when necessary, and helps them develop their talents professionally. By investing in her people, Cindy has built a highly effective team; every member excels in their areas of expertise.

Cindy used her pregnancy center service experience to grow Care Net's Pregnancy Decision Line in both size and effectiveness in reaching people considering abortion. She led the development of *Compassion, Hope, and Help*, Care Net's signature training curriculum for pregnancy center client advocates, and she oversaw content development for the *Making Life Disciples* curriculum, designed to equip people of faith to provide life-affirming, long-term discipleship to others in their churches and beyond. And, believing that investing in people is investing in the future of the pregnancy center movement, Cindy has overseen a massive project to make Care Net training available digitally through its Centers of Excellence University.

Cindy has also taught hundreds of pregnancy center leaders the principles of servant leadership, helping them be truly effective at serving and empowering others in ministry.

Today, Cindy is thriving in her role as a servant leader at Care Net. She adores her team and often says, "It's easy to be a leader of leaders as we serve our Care Net affiliates together." And, with twenty-twenty hindsight, Cindy understands that all along God was working in her life to prepare her "for such a time as this."

Cindy is thankful that the pregnancy center ministry is full of servant leaders with hearts for people. And she is thankful that her friend who chose abortion all those years ago has forgiven Cindy for her clumsy attempts to help. But mostly, Cindy is thankful that her friend has claimed for herself the hope and forgiveness offered by the greatest leader of all—Jesus Christ.

In 2020, Regent University inducted Cindy into its School of Business and Leadership Alumni Hall of Distinction. Acknowledging her tireless service on behalf of the unborn, Regent stated that she embodies the very essence of the university's mission and values: "Christian leadership to change the world." Seeking always to serve like Jesus, Cindy inspires the entire Care Net family, not only in all she does, but in who she is—a servant leader. To him be the glory!

LEADERSHIP INSIGHT

*Teach me to do your will, for you are my God; may your good
Spirit lead me on level ground.*

—Psalm 143:10

Cindy's goal was never to lead nor to become great. She just wanted to be and to do what God wanted.

Jesus said in Matthew 20:26b, "Whoever wants to become great among you must be your servant." As Martin Luther King Jr. said, "Everybody can be great because everybody can serve." And serving has made Cindy a great leader.

Walking down the road God placed her on, Cindy kept following her desire to serve those struggling with unplanned pregnancies—and that road led to leadership. Then, her heart to lead like Jesus—"just as the Son of Man did not come to be served, but to serve, and to give his life . . . for many" (Matthew 20:28)—led Cindy to servant leadership.

> Seeking what God wants you to be and do, serving others, and walking the path God puts you on is the way to true greatness. And a heart to be like Jesus is the only way to servant leadership.

LET'S PRAY:

Father, we thank you for Jesus. Thank you that he came to serve and to give his life for us. Give us hearts to be like him. Guide us as we walk down the road you place before us and empower us to serve like Jesus. We commit our lives to servant leadership as we lead for life. Amen.

HOW DO YOU LIVE IT?

1. What stands out to you from Cindy's story that makes her a fantastic leader?

2. How did Jesus show servant leadership?

3. Why is it important to be a servant leader?

GOD WRITES YOUR STORY, TOO

Now may the God of peace . . . equip you with everything good for doing his will, and may he work in us what is pleasing to him, through Jesus Christ, to whom be glory for ever and ever. Amen.

—Hebrews 13:20–21

Through these leading-for-life stories, we have received a taste of God's great movement for life across America. We have journeyed with these leaders through their struggles and their victories. We have been with them in their encounters with God. And we have rejoiced at what God has accomplished through them.

Now, take a few minutes to reflect on the characteristics that God gave them to equip them for leadership. As you meditate on his-story within their stories and how he equipped them with everything good to do his will, listen for him to speak to you.

PRIORITIZING JESUS: SOL PITCHON

Prioritizing Jesus can change your life. In fact, if you are to be the leader your team needs, it *must* change you.

PASSION: ANDY MERRITT

Cling to God, and passion for him will fulfill your calling and destiny; he will receive the glory.

VISION AND OBEDIENCE: RAUL AND CHRISTINE REYES

Leaders must be obedient to "Go," take a stand against the devil's schemes, and follow God's vision.

HOPE: GWEN KIK

As a leader, you must help build a bridge for grieving clients to cross over to the giver of hope.

TRUTH: CANDY GIBBS

Leaders are called to love people unconditionally and share God's truth unashamedly.

LOVING AND CARING: ANNE PIERSON

The best leaders inspire others through loving and caring for them.

FAITH: JIM SPRAGUE

Leaders live by faith, serve by faith, and lead by faith. Your faith will be made complete by your actions.

HUMILITY: MARY LEQUIEU

Depend on God's power—not on human wisdom—to bring you a team and fully equip you for leadership.

COMPASSION: YVONNE WILLIAMS

Leaders are called to pay forward with compassion the comfort given them by the Father of compassion.

SERVANT LEADERSHIP: CINDY HOPKINS

Leading like Jesus is the only way to servant leadership.

YOU ARE GOD'S STORY

We praise God for your calling and your God-given leadership characteristics. It is our prayer that you have learned from the experiences and the leadership characteristics exemplified by these women and men. We hope you have been encouraged and inspired by God's transformational power in the stories of their lives, their life-affirming work, and their leadership.

As a leader, you might be driven to accomplish much. That can be good if your passion to do comes from a place of spiritual health. It can be detrimental—not only to you but to others—if accomplishment becomes what defines you and how you define your team. Remember that your worth and theirs comes from being made in God's image. God calls us to simply be—not just do. When we realize we can rest in what Jesus has done, we are like a little child who presents a crayon drawing and is delighted by the praise of their Father, while knowing they couldn't do a single thing that would make him love them any less.

When you place your life and your work in his hands, you return your Father's love and praise. **Remember that doing your best is the best you can do; but being your best is the best that God can do.**

We fervently pray that you will trust him to write your story as this pro-abundant-life movement continues and brings him glory—long into the future.

For this reason, since the day we heard about you, we have not stopped praying for you. We continually ask God to fill you with the knowledge of his will through all the wisdom and understanding that the Spirit gives, so that you may live a life worthy of the Lord and please him in every way: bearing fruit in every good work, growing in the knowledge of God.

—Colossians 1:9–10

ABOUT THE AUTHOR

Sue Fultz has served in the pro-life movement since 1998 and with Care Net as a center services specialist since 2004. As an experienced consultant, she also provides onsite training to pregnancy centers with a focus on advising and equipping boards. Sue was the founding executive director of the Two Hearts Pregnancy Care Center in Ashland, Kentucky, and its satellite, Two Hearts Pregnancy Care Center of Lawrence County, Ohio.

Sue attended the University of Kentucky and was awarded a graduate certificate in pastoral ministry by Trinity College of the Bible and Theological Seminary. She has experience in public administration and plan development in the Louisville metro area.

She became pro-life because it broke her heart that unborn babies were being destroyed. Then she began meeting the mothers and fathers of these children, and her heart broke for them, too. Finally, her heart broke when she realized that aborting babies and hurting their mothers and fathers was truly an attack on God, the giver of life.

Because abortion breaks God's heart, Sue seeks an end to it, one pregnancy decision at a time. Because she loves Jesus, she loves these babies and their families and is committed to serving for life.

You can share with Sue at: suecfultz@gmail.com

ACKNOWLEDGMENTS

God—who has done exceedingly more than I could ask or imagine in opening the door of opportunity for me to author this book, which has been the ongoing desire of my heart.

Roland Warren, CEO, Care Net—who believed in me and trusted me to author this book.

Cynthia Hopkins, Vice President of Center Services and Client Care, Care Net—my longtime friend, inspiration, and mentor, without whom this book would not be possible.

Eve Marie Barner Gleason, Affiliate Advancement Director, Care Net—who shared my vision and my journey in making this book a reality.

Godly leaders—who shared their amazing, God-inspired stories of leading for life that have advanced the kingdom of God and the pro-abundant-life movement.

Care Net Center Services Team—for allowing me to serve as center services specialist, which has given me the opportunity to hear the stories of hundreds of amazing pro-life leaders in Care Net centers across America.

David, my husband—who proofread my writing and encouraged me all along the way.

Lee Ann Bisulca, my editor at Illuminations Editing—who made this manuscript the best it could be.

ADDITIONAL RESOURCES

Interested in exploring how God wants to use you in life-affirming ministry? There's a place for you in the pro-abundant-life movement. Take a Centers of Excellence University course and discover how God wants to use you!

At church through an individual or group study

Making Life Disciples Course

In the community through a local pregnancy center

Caring Foundations Course

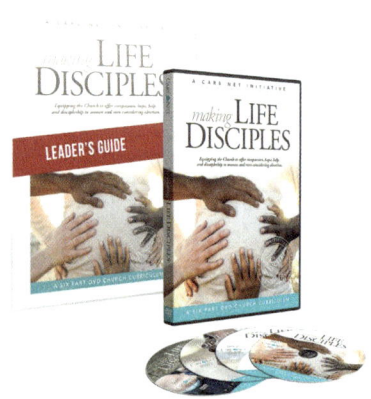

Or, share the pro-abundant-life vision with others

Why We Must Be Pro Abundant Life Booklet

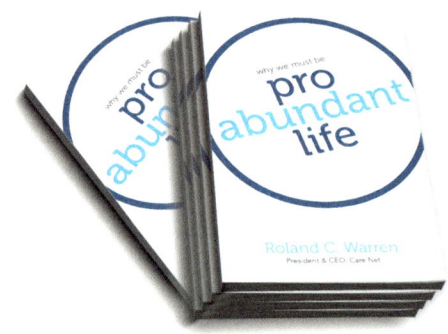